WEST PAPUA
FOLLOW THE MORNING STAR

Ben Bohane   Liz Thompson   Jim Elmslie   preface by John Rumbiak

prowling tiger press

Melbourne Australia

Prowling Tiger Press
prowling@bigpond.net.au

First published 2003
Designed by Lynne Hamilton
Edited by Cathy Edmonds
Printed by Imago, Singapore
Prepress by Digital Imaging Group, Port Melbourne

National Library of Australia
Cataloguing-in-Publication data:

West Papua follow the morning star.

ISBN 0 9586647 6 5.

1. Irian Jaya (Indonesia) - Pictorial works. 2. Irian Jaya (Indonesia) - Politics and government - 1963- . 3. Irian Jaya (Indonesia) - Social conditions. 4. Irian Jaya (Indonesia) - Social life and customs. 5. Irian Jaya (Indonesia) - Description and travel. I. Thompson, Liz, 1963- . II. Elmslie, Jim. III. Bohane, Ben, 1970- .

995.1

Archival photographs on pages 4–34 from the Netherlands Institute of War Documentation and Jos Donkers/photo-archive of the Dutch Franciscans, Utrecht, were kindly sourced by Kiki van Bilsen, Holland.

Back cover photograph: Liz Thompson
Map by Norm Robinson

Liz Thompson's work is kindly sponsored by Leica. LEICA

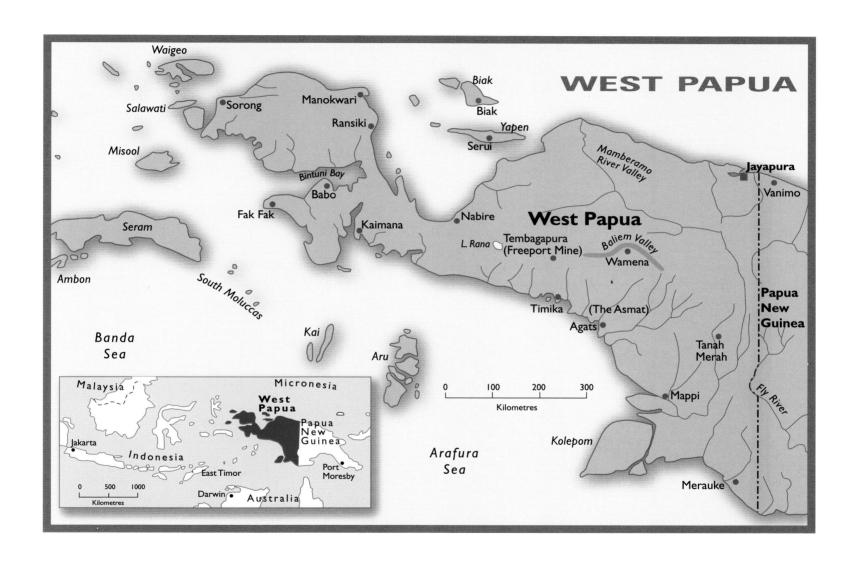

WEST PAPUA

Waigeo

Biak

Biak

Salawati

Sorong

Manokwari

Ransiki

Yapen

Mamberamo River Valley

Misool

Serui

Jayapura

Bintuni Bay

Babo

Vanimo

Fak Fak

Nabire

West Papua

Seram

Kaimana

L. Rana

Tembagapura
(Freeport Mine)

Baliem Valley

Wamena

Papua New Guinea

Ambon

South Moluccas

Kai

Timika

(The Asmat)

Agats

Aru

Tanah Merah

Banda Sea

Fly River

Mappi

Kolepom

Arafura Sea

Merauke

0   100   200   300
Kilometres

Malaysia

Micronesia

West Papua

Jakarta

Indonesia

Papua New Guinea

East Timor

Port Moresby

0   500   1000
Kilometres

Darwin

Australia

Acknowledgements

This book is the culmination of many years of travelling and learning about the country so close to Australia's shores; West Papua. It is only through the generosity and kindness of the West Papuan people that we were able to explore this vast country and experience its beauty and mystery. We thank them for sharing their lives with us. Papua Merdeka!

Special thanks to Lynne Hamilton and Patty Brown for the late nights and many emails it took to publish this book, and David Bridie for making it all possible.

We would also like to thank John Rumbiak, the Australian West Papua Association, John Ondawame, Rex Rumakiek, Bob Brown, Joe Collins, Mark Davis, Steven Feld, Matthew Jamieson, Matthew Karney, Dr Peter King, Anne Noonan, Stuart Rees and the West Papua Project at the Centre for Peace and Conflict Studies, University of Sydney, Evan Williams and Mark Worth.

Finally, thanks to the legendary Jayapura Room which hosted visiting dignitaries and degenerates in equal measure; where whisky, wit and a warm welcome greeted all.

The publisher would like to acknowledge the long hours put in by John O'Meara, Cliff Booth, Megan Ellis, Cathy Edmonds, Vanda Hamilton and Mary Callahan.

John Rumbiak is West Papua's leading human rights advocate and Director of ELS-HAM (Institute for Reliance and Human RIghts) in Jayapura. He is currently in the United States of America after receiving numerous death threats following his investigation into the shootings in August 2002 of school teachers at the Freeport mine in West Papua. (Photograph: Agence France-Presse)

West Papua
A struggle for dignity, justice and peace

In December 1994, when Amungme tribal chief Tuarek Narkime protested against the brutality of the Indonesian Armed Forces who tortured, killed and raped his people, the original owners of the land taken by the giant US-owned mining company PT Freeport Indonesia, he covered his body in mud, and wearing his penis gourd (koteka), he marched from Banti, his village, up to Freeport's company town, Tembagapura. There, Narkime told Freeport officials, 'Gentlemen, I am angry with God. Why has He created such beautiful mountains, valleys and rivers, rich with minerals and placed us—the indigenous peoples—here in this place that attracts so many people from around the world to come, exploit our resources, and kill us? You had better kill me now, kill all of my people, all our livestock, dig a big grave and bury us all, and then you can do whatever you want on our grave!' Chief Narkime was my mentor, my inspiration. He once said to me, 'I know Freeport and the military have created so many problems for us. But our minds and hearts have to be as clean and white as the Nemangkawiarat (white arrow, the Amungme name for the glacier-capped Carstenz mountain peak) when you fight for truth and justice for your people and land.'

Narkime's words and actions exemplify the best elements and principles of the Papuans' struggle: integrity, nonviolent direct action, and compassion.

They are themes that infuse hundreds of years of experience in which Papuans, from the coastal areas to the mountain highlands, have resisted foreign colonisation and domination by traders, missionaries, governments and multinational corporations. Here are some examples of the struggle in its many facets. In Manokwari in 1855, the people of Dorei resisted two German missionaries, Ottow and Geissler, sent by Zending Netherlandsche Heerforme de Kirkie (ZNHK) to introduce Christianity to the area.

Geissler and Ottow pursued their mission by destroying and degrading the culture and identity of the Dorei people, inducing them to accept the new religion. In 1943, the Biak people founded the Koreri (freedom) movement, peacefully protesting against the military occupation of Biak Island during which the Japanese killed hundreds of local people. For more than three decades, the Amungme and Kamoro peoples in the Timika area of Papua have resisted Freeport, the corporate/military giant that is decapitating their sacred mountains, destroying their rivers and rainforests, displacing their communities, and decimating their local economies and cultures.

And since the 1960s, Papuans have been fighting against the occupation of their land by Indonesia. Papuans believe that the UN-supervised and American-backed process by which the Netherlands ceded control of Papua to Indonesia violated international legal protections of the rights to self-determination, to governance by Papuans themselves over their natural resources, and to development. Indonesian occupation of Papua has brought a million migrants to the territory as well as large-scale natural resource extraction operations that have displaced and marginalised indigenous Papuans and torn the social fabric of their communities. Human rights activists have reported that an estimated 100,000 Papuans have lost their lives in resisting Indonesia's occupation. In the face of so much suffering, Papuans have committed themselves to pursuing a peaceful movement towards their goal: FREEDOM. The Papua Presidium Council (PDP) founded by Papuans in June 2000 to lead this struggle, believe that only through peaceful dialogue can the Papuan case be resolved. Their commitment to a path of nonviolence has held strong, even as the Indonesian military has assassinated PDP chairman and community leader Theys H. Eluay (10 November 2001) and mounted a campaign of terror and intimidation against Papuans from the PDP leadership to human rights defenders and the church to the grassroots. In its newest phase, Papuans in civil service and civil society are now actively seeking to establish Papua as a 'Land of Peace,' a violence-free zone in which all people and the natural environment can thrive.

One may wonder, what really is the Papuan struggle? It is a struggle for dignity, justice and peace for all. This is not the struggle of Papuans alone, but also of those—no matter who they are or where they are in the world—who share similar values, who believe in respect for other human beings and their cultures and in respect and reverence for this beautiful natural planet on which we all depend for life. The struggle of the Papuans is a challenge to those who consider themselves to be civilised, to be the proponents of modern society, who worship big capital and who are the keepers of 'sophisticated' modern knowledge. The Papuan struggle offers an educational opportunity to those who have lost their spiritual connections to nature and to other human beings. It is a struggle for everyone living or who will ever live in Papua.

This book, written by Liz Thompson, Jim Elmslie and Ben Bohane, gives you insights into Papua, into the core issues of both sides of Papua's story: history, oppression and exploitation of the people and their natural resources on the one hand, but also the beauty of Papua, its people and their culture on the other. These are the truths of the Papuans' struggle today.

John Rumbiak
New York City
December 2002

Jim Elmslie

West Papua is a land in crisis and despair. The Melanesian people of West Papua believe that their very existence is under grave threat. Since 1963 they have been under the control of the Indonesian government, which has resulted in widespread dispossession, marginalisation, torture and the deaths of tens of thousands of people.[1] This process is continuing today. In fact, the situation is deteriorating as the awesome economic resources of West Papua are targeted for more intense exploitation—not only the mineral, oil and gas deposits found across the island, but also the virgin forests for logging, the seas for fishing, and major river systems for dams to provide electricity and industrial development. These resources are vast—the Freeport gold and copper mine is the most valuable in the world, while US$20 billion worth of oil and gas has already been discovered. The desperate quest of the impoverished Indonesian state to exploit these resources puts the lives of the West Papuans at great risk. Like so many other indigenous people throughout the world, they are staring down the gun barrel of economic development gone out of control.

West Papua is the western half of the island of New Guinea, which lies just to the north of Australia: the other half of the island is Papua New Guinea (PNG). The island is dominated by a long ridge of mountains running east–west, rising to above 5000 metres. On the northern and southern coasts are flood plains of silt washed down as the mountains are eroded by the high rainfall caused by the rain trap of the central highlands. The Melanesian people have been living on the island of New Guinea for approximately 50,000 years. It is the oldest cultivating society in existence.

There are about 270 tribal languages spoken in West Papua, reflecting the diversity of the culture and terrain. Traditionally these people had little contact with the rest of humanity except annual honggi raids that were carried out by the forces of the Sultan of Tidore, based in the famous spice islands near Halmahera to the north-west of New Guinea. The north coast was raided almost every year for slaves and plunder. There was also trade in bird of paradise skins, and other contacts with the Indonesians to the west; however, it is fair to say that the vast majority of the Melanesians of New Guinea, including West Papua, were completely in charge of their own lives until very recently.

West Papua began to be absorbed into the Dutch East Indies empire when the Dutch signed a treaty with the Sultan of Tidore in 1660. The Sultan, because of the honggi raids, claimed West Papua as part of his domain; however, that would have been a great surprise to most West Papuans. The Dutch claimed formal possession in 1828 to delineate the eastern extremity of their empire. They took little interest in their acquisition, which seemed to have few resources that they could exploit. Colonial presence was minimal throughout the

[1] For further elaboration on this and other points in this chapter see *Irian Jaya Under The Gun; Indonesian Economic Development Versus West Papuan Nationalism* by Jim Elmslie. University of Hawaii Press, Honolulu, 2002.

Papuan warrior from the Merauke region
in South New Guinea, an area known for its
cannibalistic rituals. (1943)

19th century and until 1926 when a revolt in Java against Dutch rule was put down and political prisoners were sent to Boven-Digoel, a camp in West Papua. Prior to the second world war Dutch colonial interest remained very low. All this changed after the war and the Japanese occupation as Indonesian nationalists fought the returning Dutch in their quest for independence.

In 1949, following four years of armed conflict, Holland surrendered control over all the regions of the Dutch East Indies empire except for West New Guinea. The Dutch retained control of West New Guinea in the hope of allowing this portion of the empire to become independent in its own right. Holland argued that there was little or no connection between the Asian Indonesians and the Melanesian West Papuans, and that West Papua was physically located in Melanesia, not Asia. The Dutch also hoped to exploit the resources of a separate, independent West New Guinea and to extract themselves from 300 years of brutal empire with some semblance of dignity. In the 1949 settlement the Dutch specifically did not commit to any ultimate political future for West New Guinea, although the Indonesians went away from the agreement assuming that West New Guinea would join the rest of Indonesia within a year. Talks on the issue failed to take place and a dangerous limbo situation developed wherein the Dutch laid the groundwork for a West Papuan nation with independence to be achieved in 1971.

Meanwhile, Indonesian rhetoric laying claim to the province intensified. This process was brought to a head in 1961 when President Sukarno ordered the invasion of West Papua. Operation Mandala, under the command of General Suharto, commenced: 1500 Indonesian paratroopers were dropped into West Papua to attack the Dutch. At sea, naval confrontations occurred around Aru Bay. These military clashes were victories for the Dutch, but, even as they achieved some success on the battlefield, Holland was progressively undermined on the world political stage. The crucial element in this turnaround occurred in 1960 when the Russian government gave a 'soft loan' to the Indonesian government of US$450 million to aid Indonesia's military build-up in response to Dutch intransigence over the West Papua issue.

To compensate for his lack of a firm political base President Sukarno sought cooperation from, but promoted rivalry between, the Indonesian Communist Party (PKI) and the Indonesian military (ABRI)—the two most powerful institutions within Indonesian society. Sukarno tempered the political might of the military by allowing the PKI to have a powerful, but not dominant, role in Indonesian politics. However, with the loan from the Russians, the United States of America became concerned that Indonesia was moving into the global communist camp. The issue of West Papua, therefore, became embroiled in cold war geo-politics. The Indonesian government used the concerns of the Americans to gain their support against the Dutch over West Papua. The Americans began to back the Indonesian view because they saw it as essential to keep Indonesia out of the communist camp and were prepared to sacrifice the future of the West Papuans for that end. Once America had swung its support behind Indonesia, Australia, which had been a supporter of either independence or amalgamation of West Papua with a future independent Papua New Guinea, dropped its support for the Dutch position. The Dutch, therefore, were left either to confront the Indonesians half-way across the world entirely on their own or accept Indonesian occupation. In August 1962 they chose the latter course.

In defeat, the Dutch signed the New York Agreement which allowed for a United Nations Temporary Executive Authority (UNTEA) to take over administration of West Papua. Under the terms of the agreement the people of West Papua retained their right to self-determination, in effect by the opportunity to 'exercise freedom of choice' to ascertain the 'will of the population' as to whether to be incorporated into Indonesia or not.[2] The actual mechanism of determining the will of the people was left deliberately vague, except that it should be carried out 'in accordance with international practice'.[3] This vagueness stemmed from the fact that Indonesian agreement to some form of self-determination allowed a face-saving compromise for the Dutch and resolved the issue from the point of view of the United Nations (UN). There was no mention of the words 'referendum' or 'plebiscite' in the New York Agreement and no real hope that the rights of the West Papuans would be respected—but the diplomatic niceties had been observed and war between Holland and Indonesia was averted.

UNTEA remained in control until May 1963 when the 1500 UN troops who had monitored the Dutch withdrawal moved out and passed administration over to the Indonesians. The Indonesian government was obliged by the terms of the New York Agreement to hold a consultation with the West Papuan people within five years of this handover date. However, in 1965 Sukarno withdrew from the UN as part of his confrontation with Malaysia. Konfrontasi was a military adventure designed to ward off attention from the large-scale economic, social and political crisis in which Indonesia found itself. Sukarno claimed that, not being a member of the UN, Indonesia was no longer obliged to hold any sort of consultation. The issue of West Papua was put aside.

This situation changed, however, with the September 1965 coup and counter-coup in Jakarta when General Suharto seized power. Suharto's new government wished to rejoin the UN, which meant that they were again obliged to hold a consultation over West Papua's political status. Thus, a consultation was finally held in 1969—the infamous UN-sponsored Act of Free Choice. The Indonesians maintained that the Papuan people were too backward to allow a 'one man, one vote' election, so they constructed a process whereby 1026 'community leaders' were hand-picked and, under severe coercion, forced to vote unanimously for incorporation into Indonesia.

[2] John Saltford, *The United Nations and the Indonesian Takeover of West Papua, 1962–1969: The Anatomy of Betrayal*, RoutledgeCurzon, London, 2003.
[3] ibid.

A coastal village of stilt huts, part of the Dutch East Indies colonial empire, north New Guinea. (1929)

Though widely considered a sham at the time, it has recently been exposed that even the UN officials who oversaw the vote considered it a betrayal of the West Papuan people. 'It was just a whitewash. The mood at the United Nations was to get rid of this problem as quickly as possible,' said Chakravarthy Narasimhan, a retired UN undersecretary-general who handled the vote.[4]

The vote, however, was the condition laid down by the UN for Indonesia's readmission into the organisation, and the UN accepted the outcome of the Act of Free Choice because the two principal players, Indonesia and Holland, already had. Head of the UN mission sent to monitor the vote, Fernando Ortiz Sanz, though with grave personal misgivings as to the veracity of the 'vote', presented his final report in November 1969 which stated that 'an act of free choice has taken place in West Irian (West Papua) in accordance with Indonesian practice, in which the representatives of the population have expressed their wish to remain with Indonesia'.[5] This was in the face of comments from objective observers that the overwhelming majority of Papuans were against being incorporated into Indonesia. The report was noted by the United Nations General Assembly by 84 votes to none, with 30 abstentions. Sovereignty over West Papua finally passed to Indonesia. Resentment and repression have endured ever since.

Stark differences exist between Indonesians from an Asian background and West Papuan Melanesians. The traditional dress of the diverse West Papuan tribal groups, especially in the interior, jars the sensibilities of many Indonesians. They find bare breasts and men wearing only penis gourds offensive, and the tribal people are consequently viewed as 'backward'. The predominantly Muslim Indonesians view pigs as unclean and foul creatures, while to Melanesian people they are the highest form of wealth. The West Papuan people are also overwhelmingly Christian—more so as the oppression against them has increased. Some Indonesians see the West Papuan people as infidels and non-believers and a threat to the purity of the largest Muslim nation on earth. The differences between the Melanesian West Papuans and the Muslim Indonesians have not ameliorated with time: in fact, they have become exacerbated as Indonesian misrule has intensified the West Papuans' feelings of betrayal and dispossession.

The West Papuan view that a fundamental injustice had been visited upon them was expressed right from the first Indonesian presence, in the form of large-scale uprisings mounted against the Indonesian military forces in the mid-1960s in the Paniai region; in the Baliem Valley; near Manokwari; and to a lesser extent across the entire province. All these uprisings were singularly unsuccessful, because large numbers of unarmed or very poorly armed demonstrators confronted heavily armed and trained troops who quite easily quelled them.

[4] Slobodan Lekic, 'Historic vote was sham, ex-UN chiefs admit', *Sydney Morning Herald*, 23 November 2001.
[5] Saltford, op. cit.

But in the 1970s, even after Indonesian sovereignty had been recognised by the UN and the issue of West Papua had faded from the attention of the rest of the world, opposition to the Indonesians continued: large-scale uprisings, however, became less common, as it became obvious that this form of rebellion was unsuccessful. Opposition became clandestine and continued in remote areas.

Organisasi Papua Merdeka, the Free West Papua movement, or OPM, grew out of these early uprisings in the 1960s and developed into a bush-based network of poorly armed insurgents confronting the state. Relatively small units of guerrillas, numbering less than 100, attached to various camps such as Markus Victoria and Markus Pemka near the PNG border, lived in the jungle of thick dense bush and rainforest, avoiding the Indonesian military and conducting occasional raids or armed attacks against the Indonesians. By 1971 the OPM was under the command of Jacob Prai, who had been a law student at Cenderawasih University in Jayapura, the capital of Irian Jaya, until he found it impossible to live with the regime and took to the bush. He was joined by another West Papuan, Seth Rumkorem, who had been in the Indonesian army as an intelligence officer until he reacted against continuous discrimination. Rumkorem, as a trained soldier, reorganised the OPM into a more cohesive fighting unit which, although hopelessly out-numbered, continued to provide for all West Papuans a sense that the opposition which they felt in their hearts, but which could not be openly expressed, was echoed by the OPM's presence in the bush.

The Indonesian government felt that West Papuan nationalism had emerged only on Dutch initiatives to begin the process whereby West Papua would become an independent state. The Indonesians thought that the Dutch policy of preparing West Papua for independence was irresponsible because it created false expectations within the West Papuan community. It was assumed that with time the West Papuans would overcome this mindset and accept that they were actually Indonesian subjects. With some West Papuans this did undoubtedly occur; they thought that the prospect of independence had become so remote that they should accept their position and do what they could within a struggling and faulty third-world society, rather than risk their lives pursuing the dream of a free state. The punishment for pursuing this dream was great; for instance in 1988 Dr Thomas Wainggai was sentenced to 20 years jail for flying an independence flag at a demonstration in Jayapura. (His Japanese-born wife was sentenced to eight years for sewing the flag.)

The last large-scale uprising against Indonesian rule occurred in 1984 when more than 100 West Papuan members of the Indonesian army defected with their weapons and attempted a mutiny against the state. However, the Indonesian military had been forewarned and pre-empted the mutineers, cracking down on known OPM supporters. Thousands fled across the border to PNG, which by the end of 1985 had accepted some 10,000 West Papuan refugees in camps dotted along the border. This seemingly futile rebellion appeared to be the last gasp of the OPM for most outside observers; however, the dream of independence did not die. In fact, it seemed to grow

Part of the glacier and ice-capped mountain that towers 5000 metres above the Freeport mine. (Photograph: Jim Elmslie)

Freeport mine from the air, one of the world's largest mining operations, grinding down the mountains of West Papua. (Photograph: Jim Elmslie)

in an almost religious manner, as people more than ever came to associate independence with an ideal future where somehow all the problems of the Papuans would be solved.

In the 1980s Indonesia was under the secure authoritarian rule of President Suharto at the height of his power. It was a society that tolerated no dissent and where Suharto and his clique seemed to be at the peak of every power structure. Economic growth had been spectacular over 25 years of the New Order regime which had delivered solid improvements in people's living conditions, health levels and education. These benefits did not assuage the feelings of the West Papuans; however, as there was no forum for them to vent their anger, the cries of protest remained stifled. The situation appeared to have calmed to such an extent that the OPM was written off as a political force, and dismissed as a gang of bandits numbering less than 100. West Papuan nationalism was widely considered to be dead.

The population profile of the country was changing rapidly, as well. Indonesians, either government-sponsored transmigrants or enterprising 'spontaneous migrants', flooded into the province escaping poverty and hoping for a better existence than that on offer in overcrowded western Indonesia. Settling predominantly in urban areas or specially created transmigration camps these new settlers are another threat to the Melanesian West Papuans because they are a distinctly different racial and religious group, and because they compete for land, resources and jobs. In the camps and in the cities the migrants already make up a clear majority of the population, resulting in discrimination against the Melanesians. While Melanesians still represent a majority in the population of 2.3 million, and an overwhelming majority in much of the remote inland, if the present demographic trends continue they will soon be a minority, with all that that entails. Transmigration was partly funded by the World Bank and promoted as 'development'; yet in locations across the country it has created only dispossession and marginalisation for the original occupants.

Until the mid-1990s very little information emerged from the province because of the inability of the local people to write or broadcast about their living conditions and the physical conditions in which they found themselves, and because very few outsiders came to visit. Those who did come were overwhelmingly concerned with exploiting the vast natural resources, particularly the Freeport copper and gold concession in the south of the country, in what is perhaps the richest geological area on the face of the planet. Freeport began as a fairly small mine in the 1960s and the United States owner/operators developed very close links to the Suharto regime. Freeport, in fact, was the very first foreign investment project signed after General Suharto took power in Indonesia. PT Freeport Indonesia prospered under his guardianship and expanded its operations as a significant producer of copper from the Grasberg deposit near the town of Tembagapura in the central mountains above the Asmat swamp.

In 1990 a second deposit at Ertsberg was discovered, only three kilometres from Grasberg. The deposit was 33 times larger than the original copper and gold deposit and led to a major expansion of the mine operations. The Concession of Work area grew from 10,000 to 2.5 million hectares—25,000 square kilometres of a total of 414,000 square kilometres for the whole of West Papua. The Amungme and Kamoro people, whose traditional lands are used by the mine site and in the associated support operations, are severely affected by the mine's presence and by the military repression which enables the mine to continue its operations in the face of local opposition. On many occasions Amungme and Kamoro people have been killed by security forces for protesting against the mine. Many of the mountain people have also been moved down to the lowlands where they have little resistance to malaria and other diseases, and have died as a result.

Although it was attacked in 1977, the situation at the mine appeared quite secure until the mid-1990s when reliable information started to emerge from the province of killings that had occurred around Christmas 1994. A local pastor and members of his congregation were gunned down by ABRI troops pursuing OPM members who had conducted a series of flag-raisings in the valleys around the concession. This information was released in an Australian Council for Overseas Aid (ACFOA) report, telling for the first time victims' names and where, when and by whom they had been killed. The report required comment by the Indonesian government.

Jakarta initially rejected all allegations; however, this prompted the Catholic Church in Jayapura to conduct its own investigation. Bishop Munninghoff, head of the Catholic Church in West Papua, subsequently released a report that largely confirmed the ACFOA report and the number of people killed, but specifically did not examine Freeport's role in the military operations other than to note that it was part of Freeport's contract to house and provide for the soldiers operating in its area. The OPM attacks perhaps had their genesis in the expansion of the mine's concession area as people in surrounding highland regions feared that the mine's operations would expand into their own areas and subject them to the same process that had befallen the Amungme. The upshot of these reports was a level of media interest in West Papua that had not been experienced since the 1984 uprisings.

East of Freeport in the Mapenduma region, the OPM Southern Command was under the control of veteran OPM guerrilla fighter Kelly Kwalik, who had been in the bush fighting the Indonesians for over 20 years. In early 1996 his command kidnapped a group of British, Dutch, German and Indonesian scientists who were conducting a fauna survey in the Lorenz National Park. This hostage crisis dragged on for four months before an ABRI raid which resulted in the OPM killing two of the Indonesian hostages and the successful rescue of all the Europeans. This four-month period focused West Papua in the international spotlight as never before and the high level of oppression became much better known. The fact that the OPM existed and that West Papuan nationalism was alive could no longer be denied by the Indonesian government or outside observers.

Coming face to face with new technology, Dutch New Guinea. (1938)

Throughout 1996 there were demonstrations and uprisings in Jayapura, the Baliem Valley, Timika and elsewhere. Once again these demonstrations and riots were brought under control by the military, but they did have the effect of spreading consciousness throughout West Papua and the South Pacific region, that West Papua nationalism, instead of declining and disappearing, was in fact growing and intensifying. This situation—increasingly open calls for independence—gained momentum in early 1997 and 1998 as the economic situation in Indonesia deteriorated sharply and political and social instability increased. For the first time in decades, the Suharto regime was under threat.

The Asian economic crisis was brought on by a frenzy of foreign money being pumped into the Asian 'tiger' and would-be 'tiger' economies. South-East Asia was perceived to be following the same path as Japan and enjoying rapid economic development and growth. However, much of the money ended up in speculative investments and real estate, creating short-term booms which were unsustainable. Most of the funds being poured into the region came from short-term loans designated in US dollars. When the bubble inevitably burst in 1997, the foreign money was withdrawn and Thailand, Korea and subsequently Indonesia were thrown into economic turmoil. These countries all suffered real estate and share market collapses and their currencies rapidly devalued against the US dollar. The situation was exacerbated by the panic that spread amongst foreign merchant bankers, who dumped investments in a desperate bid to retrieve their funds, driving markets even lower and devastating good and bad companies alike. Greed had turned to fear as the prevailing sentiment. As the Indonesian rupiah fell to 16,000 to the US dollar (from a rate of approximately 2000 before the crisis), even well-run companies found that the value of their debts (denominated in US dollars) exceeded the value of their assets (denominated in Indonesian rupiah). Economic prosperity, the main foundation of Suharto's legitimacy to rule, crumbled. As a result, Suharto found that his previous almost unquestioned power was under challenge.

In May 1998 Suharto was finally forced to resign in the face of huge student protests in Jakarta and elsewhere, and because the International Monetary Fund (IMF) and the World Bank were no longer prepared to bail him out. The IMF, in particular, would not give more money to the Indonesian government to continue its system of 'crony' patronage and subsidies which lay at the very heart of Suharto's economic and political power. The IMF took this view because in the post-cold war era it was no longer necessary to prop up third-world dictators merely because they were anti-communist. Suharto had been valuable to the West, and particularly the US, due to his violent repression of communism. He had risen to power in a bloody coup and counter-coup episode that resulted in the deaths of hundreds of thousands of Indonesian communists and other dissidents. The Indonesian communist party was completely destroyed and the much feared 'domino effect' (whereby communism spread out from China and Russia, contaminating one country after another) was halted. Suharto was seen as a loyal ally of the anti-communist Western countries and his brutality, excesses and extreme corruption were tolerated for that reason. However, by the mid-1990s he had outlived his usefulness to the West and the conditions demanded by the IMF in exchange for urgently needed loans effectively stripped Suharto of his economic, and subsequently political, power. As this loss of Western support became clear within Indonesia, Suharto's power base rapidly shrank and the students and other disgruntled citizens were able to topple the once invincible dictator.

It was assumed that a process of democratisation would occur within Indonesia, with the students at the vanguard. In light of this, the Australian Prime Minister, John Howard, attempted to help the new Indonesian President, former Vice-President B. J. Habibie, to 'solve' the issue of East Timor. The illegal occupation of East Timor was widely seen as the major obstacle to Indonesia playing a role in global politics commensurate with its size—by population the fourth largest country in the world. Australia suggested a referendum on East Timor's future with political independence as one option. This was viewed by all parties (except the East Timorese) as the least best outcome. The suggestion was adopted by Habibie even though he viewed it as a betrayal by Australia, which was one of the very few countries that had recognised Indonesian sovereignty over East Timor. Habibie responded angrily that if the East Timorese wanted a referendum on independence it would be better sooner rather than later. He considered East Timor a drag on the finances of Indonesia and did not want to waste money on the province if it was to ultimately become an independent state. This was quite contrary to what Howard had envisaged—he had foreseen a long period of autonomy and political development and then a referendum in 10 or more years. His intention had been to defuse the issue, and help Indonesia's fuller integration into the international community by removing the odious stigma of its being a brutal occupying power. Quite the opposite occurred.

The East Timorese voted by four to one for independence and subsequently suffered the full anger and violence of the Indonesian state and military, that withdrew from the province after destroying virtually everything that could be destroyed and killing hundreds, if not thousands, of people. East Timor was, however, set on its path for independence.

This process gave a huge morale boost to the West Papuan people. The rhetoric on East Timor for 25 years had been that it would never be independent, that there was little support for independence and that it was inalienably a part of Indonesia. Yet the situation had changed rapidly; an independent East Timor had emerged and the West Papuans now felt that they could undertake a similar makeover. In response to this, President Abdurrahman Wahid, elected in 1999 as Habibie's successor, attempted to negotiate with West Papuan nationalists and address the issue of self-determination through dialogue rather than military repression. Wahid helped finance a large meeting of all the diverse West Papuan interests in May–June 2000. The Kongres Rakyat Papua II, or Congress as this meeting was called, was held in Jayapura with Wahid contributing A$172,000 towards costs on the understanding that independence would not be declared. He encouraged the participants to express their grievances but also to accept that West Papua was inextricably part of Indonesia.

At the Congress the leader of its Presidium, Chief Theys Eluay, mentioned that he did not intend to declare independence because he considered West Papua already independent—indeed, that it had been independent since 1961. In his view this claim referred back to the Dutch period when the Niew Guinee Raad (New Guinea Council) had been democratically formed and designed to take the country to independence. Theys and the Congress declared that West Papua was already free but that the country was illegally occupied by the Indonesians and had been for 40 years. This outcome was met with rapturous applause by the West Papuans, outrage by the Indonesian government and cold fury by the Indonesian military which saw its key role as being to hold the nation together at any cost.

Vice-President Megawati Sukarnoputri visited West Papua just before the Congress to observe the West Papuan independence movement at first hand. She returned to Jakarta to talk with military leaders on how to deal with the West Papuan nationalists. The outcome of this was a secret plan circulated in June 2000 which recommended a multi-pronged approach to eliminating West Papuan nationalism. Part of this plan was to infiltrate the OPM on many levels to gain information in order to discredit and distort their policies. It was also planned to intimidate, arrest and eventually murder the leaders of the movement. Chief Theys and most of the senior Presidium leadership were arrested and charged with sedition. The flying of the Morning Star flag, which had been allowed under President Wahid's new approach, was again banned. Across the province, however, flags continued to be flown as people refused to obey the government. This ultimately led to many violent confrontations, the worst being in the Baliem Valley where two men were shot while trying to stop police from removing a flag. Rioting subsequently broke out and 40 people were killed, including many Indonesian settlers who were hacked to death by Dani tribesmen and others.

The Indonesian military presence continued to grow as the crackdown on separatists spread. By 1 December 2000, which is traditionally a day of celebration for West Papuan independence, some 39 naval vessels were off the coast of Jayapura and thousands of troops had been landed throughout the region for sweeps against OPM fighters and separatists. Once again, military repression caused refugees to flee to PNG and resulted in the arrests of many student activists, two of whom were subsequently beaten to death in the police cells of Jayapura—even though a European journalist was sharing a cell with the men and witnessed one of the killings first-hand.

In 2001 the West Papuan independence movement was still being represented by the Papuan Presidium Council even though many of the leaders were in detention or under house arrest. The situation appeared to be deteriorating as civil freedoms were more and more restricted. The official Indonesian response to the unrest in the province was the implementation in October 2001 of 'special autonomy' (*Otonomi Khusus* or *Otsus*). This was seen by the Indonesian government as giving genuine concessions to the Papuans, particularly economic, but ruling out the idea of independence. The name of the province was officially changed to Papua and a much greater share of the revenue from natural resource extraction was to be returned to the province. Plans were announced for a Papuan-only Papuan

Chief Theys Eluay. (photograph: Agence France-Presse)

House of Representatives (DPRD) and for the establishment of a Commission for Truth and Reconciliation. However, most Papuans viewed *Otsus* with suspicion and disdain, if not outright contempt. In a land ruled by a corrupt military with no independent legal system, such legislation counted for little on the ground. Some even viewed it as being worse than direct-rule from Jakarta. More money in the provincial budget just provided the military/political elite who run the province further opportunity for graft and theft. It could be argued that if *Otsus* was properly implemented and transparently administrated it would be a step forward for the Papuan people—however, the level of cynicism towards the Indonesian state, borne out of decades of experience, is such that few Papuans have any faith in the state being able to deliver. Rather *Otsus* is widely ignored and the demands for independence continue.

In the midst of this increasing repression, further economic developments continue unabated. In the Bintuni Bay area some US$20 billion of gas reserves were confirmed at the Tungguh LNG resource, while on Gag Island, off the north-west coast, the world's third largest nickel and cobalt deposit is about to be developed. BHP Billiton and PT Aneka Tambang, Indonesia's state-owned mining company, are apparently spending A$2 billion to exploit the resource, much to the concern of the residents of the tiny (56 square kilometres) island. Plans are also well under way to dam the Mamberamo River—the largest river system in the country—in a vast multi-billion dollar project to produce cheap hydro-electricity for an entire new industrial zone to be established near Sorong in the north. In all of these developments TNI keeps a close involvement.[6] While ostensibly providing security to the projects, the military is actually running a massive protection racket. As in the case of Freeport, the military extorts what it can in return for stability of a kind. Whereas previously this system was more or less under control due to the pervasive influence and domination of President Suharto, a shareholder of the mine, with Suharto's downfall the system has become anarchic. Military-engineered riots and mock OPM attacks and kidnappings are the tools that TNI uses to pressure the foreign companies.

This form of intimidation was taken to new heights on 31 August 2002 when a convoy of picnicking teachers from Freeport international school was ambushed near Tembagapura. Fourteen people were shot, three fatally, including two Americans. This was the first time that Westerners had been intentionally targeted and the killings sent shock waves through the entire mine community. The Indonesian military and the mine management immediately blamed the OPM; however, many commentators—including John Rumbiak—claim that the TNI itself orchestrated these killings.

---

[6] The TNI, Tentara Nasional Indonesia (Indonesian National Army), was created after Suharto's downfall by splitting ABRI, Angkatan Bersenjata Republik Indonesia (Armed Forces of the Republic of Indonesia), into a separate police force and army.

The genesis behind the ambush seems to be changes in US accounting practices in the wake of the Enron and other American corporate collapses. Senior management are now personally responsible for their corporate accounts, which means the millions of dollars paid to TNI as, in effect, protection money was no longer acceptable practice.[8] TNI responded with classic overkill and now the entire relationship between the military and the mine, and between the US and Indonesia is in flux. The status quo of the last three decades has shifted irrevocably with the deliberate murder of American citizens.

Conflict is continuing between the TNI and the Papuan people. In the Wasior area on the north-west coast, protests by local villagers against logging operations were crushed by Brimob (mobile police brigade) and Kopassus (army special forces) troops were sent into the region. Several troops were killed in ambushes (whether by OPM, villagers or rival police/army units is unclear) which led to army sweeps through the entire region, turning large areas into free-fire zones, and causing thousands of village people to flee for their lives. The government had made it clear that it would not allow local protests to stand in the way of economic development, such as the exploitation of oil and gas. And the soldiers made it clear that their presence was vital for economic development.

Besides direct conflict with the Indonesian military and police, a new and potentially catastrophic force has emerged across West Papua. The army-backed militant Muslim organisation Laskar Jihad (some of whose members have trained in Afghanistan and reportedly have links to Osama Bin Laden), as well as other government-sponsored militias, are arming non-Melanesian Indonesian civilians all over the country in anticipation of ethnic/religious conflict. The conflict is actually being incited and planned by the military in response to the independence movement. The Jihad forces are establishing bases in remote areas as well as urban centres. As in the case of East Timor, these forces reflect government policy aimed at crushing dissent and terrorising opponents. There is also the very real threat that a genocide is being planned to provide a 'final solution' to Indonesia's problems in West Papua, just as in East Timor when a quarter of the population was forcibly deported following the August 1999 referendum on independence. Combined with the transmigrants' (and the state's) desire for land and resources, the situation for the West Papuans is dire.

This was the situation when the June 2000 plan of repression which followed Megawati Sukarnoputri's visit to West Papua in May 2000 was leaked to the outside world. Any doubts that this plan was only rhetoric were removed on 10 November 2001, when Chief Theys was abducted on his way home from a dinner party with Indonesian army officers to celebrate Indonesian Heroes Day. He was tortured and killed. The next day his battered body was found in his abandoned vehicle, the driver having 'disappeared'.

[8] Hamish McDonald, 'Kopassus accused of Freeport ambush', *Sydney Morning Herald*, 2 November 2002.

The killing took place one month after the September 11 terrorist attacks in America. In response to the attacks President Sukarnoputri gave quick support to the American position. Given that she was the leader of the largest Muslim nation on earth, the Americans were impressed and grateful—which means that transgressions by Indonesia against its minorities will probably be overlooked. By 2002, with the decapitation of the Papua Presidium, increasing military repression and moves to prevent a serious investigation of the killing of Chief Theys, many West Papuans fear they are destined for genocide. The Indonesians have always claimed that as economic development gathers strength in West Papua relations between the Melanesian and Asian segments of the population will improve; however, the opposite is occurring and it can now be seen that economic development, instead of being the saviour of the Melanesians, is proving to be their death knell.

It is only with the intervention of outside individuals and organisations to publicise the plight of the West Papuans and support moves for the reinstatement of a peace process in Papua that restraint over the military will be achieved. It is probably only through American and Australian appreciation of the urgency of the humanitarian situation that any meaningful change will occur; but without the de-militarisation of Indonesian society, without the re-visiting of the UN-sponsored Act of Free Choice in 1969, and without the linking of human rights to foreign aid, the future for the West Papuans will be bleak indeed.

The future for Indonesia is also bleak. While most Indonesians would view the retention of West Papua within the republic as an asset it is, in fact, a major impediment to any real economic and political development. Even before the 12 October 2002 bomb blasts in Bali that killed some 190 people, mostly foreigners, Indonesia's economy was sick. Foreign investment was negative as investors sought to preserve their capital and shift operations to lower-cost countries, particularly China and Vietnam. Without foreign investment there can be no economic growth. The pervasive corruption, a legal system completely lacking any integrity and an avaricious, unaccountable and violent military means that Indonesia has become a profoundly unattractive place to do business. Yet the situation is entrenched as the reality of retaining the provinces of West Papua by force means giving the military a free hand. And while the military has a free hand, no meaningful reform is possible.

This bitter legacy of Dutch colonialism was foreseen by Indonesia's first vice-president, Mohammed Hatta. Hatta was of the view that West Papua should not be incorporated into the republic on the grounds that the Papuans were racially and religiously distinct, and that geographically West Papua was part of Melanesia, not Asia. He foresaw only trouble in keeping the republic together by brute force.

Hatta's view was not widely accepted, as Sukarno, and later Suharto, strongly argued that Indonesia included all the possessions of the former Dutch East Indies. However, by maintaining West Papua within the republic they have, unwittingly, cast the die for Indonesia's future: a dismal future of economic decline, poverty and hopelessness in a rapidly degrading natural environment.

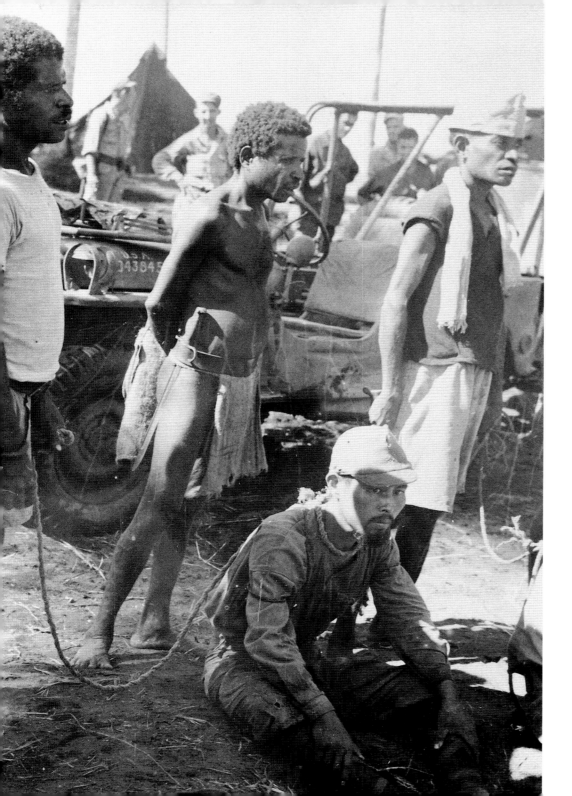

Japanese prisoners of war.

(Left to right) General Eichelberger, Lt.-Gen. L.H. van Oyen and Rear-Admiral P. Koenraad, watching Japanese P.O.W.'s at Hollandia, Netherlands New Guinea.

A section of the NEI police force, somewhere on the south-west coast of New Guinea doing preparatory exercises for fencing.

Hollandia. News is eagerly awaited by the men attached to the Royal Netherlands Navy.

The hoisting of the flag in a pioneers' bivouac. (1920)

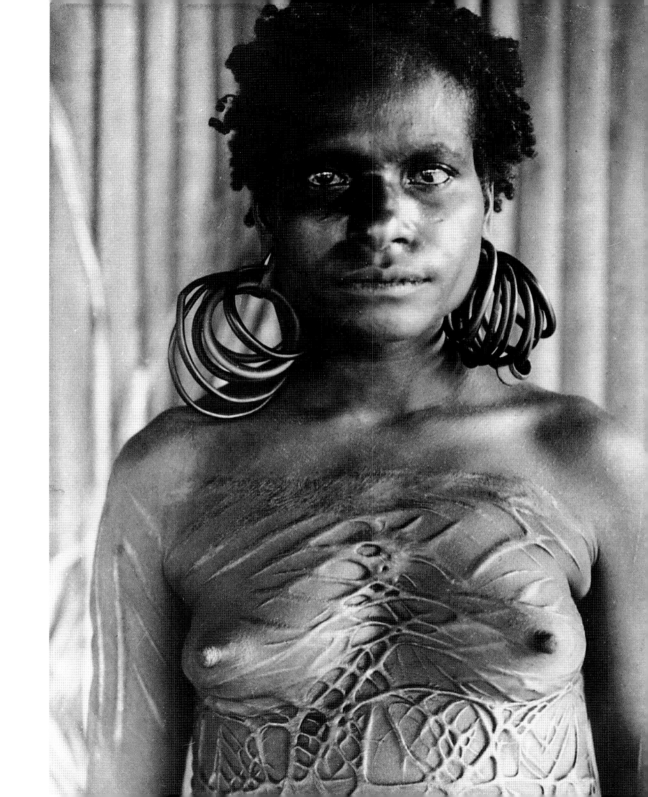

Marind-anim woman
with tattoos of scarification.

Farming lessons at a school in Kota Nica. (1955)

Astronomical topographic fixing on Hawk Island.

First contact with natives on the south coast of Netherlands New Guinea. (1943)

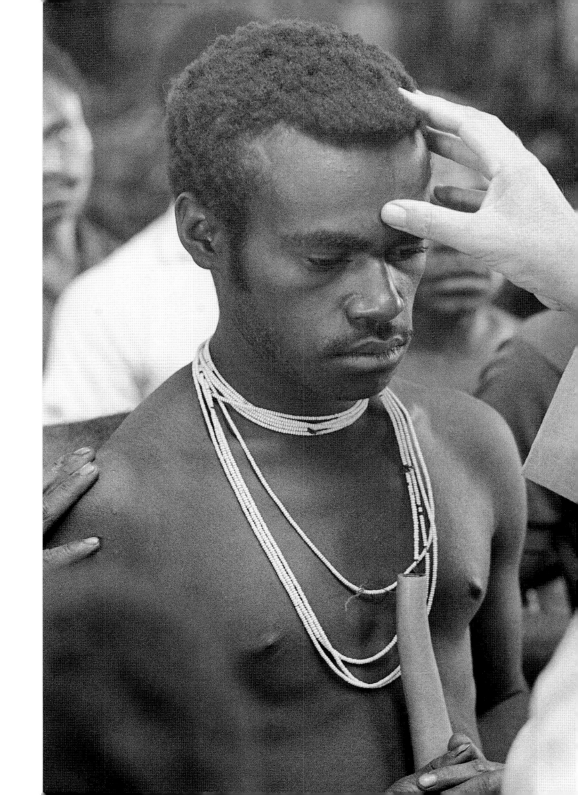

A solemn moment as a young
Papuan man absorbs the word of God.

An early Dutch missionary with Papuan women.

Spreading the word, a Dutch missionary delivers his sermon from a bush church.

A joyful meeting between a highlander and Dutch missionary nuns.

Liz Thompson

Jayapura is the capital of West Papua. The town has been built around what was known as Numbay Bay. After Indonesian occupation the area was called Yos Sudarso Bay in memory of an Indonesian navy commander. On my first visit to West Papua in the mid-1980s Suharto was in power. In numerous shops framed pictures of President Suharto hung from all available wall space, along with copies of the Pancasila or 'five principles', which is the basic text on which the moral and ethical spine of the country is based.

This statue, left, in Jayapura of Yos Sudarso depicts the Indonesian navy commander who was killed when the Dutch and Indonesian forces fought in Aru Bay. Sudarso's ship was sunk and he quickly became a national hero for his role in 'liberating' West Papua.

Jayapura is a strange assault on the senses. Flying from Vanimo in Melanesian PNG across a colonially created border which cuts through the mountainous jungle terrain, you are met, somewhat incongruously, by the bustle of Asia. Vespers career down the streets. Indonesian street vendors sell fried bean curd and pancakes filled with sweet red beans. Taxis sport furry dice hanging from the rear view mirror and posters of rippling Indonesian bodybuilders or sultry movie stars are stuck beneath heavy transparent plastic used to protect the seat covers. The markets are overflowing with Balinese fabrics, imported electrical goods and synthetic clothing. Concrete slabs are covered in shining fish, green vegetables are sprinkled with water to keep them fresh, mountains of fruit and chilli create an extraordinary array of colour. Indonesian music fills the air and the smell of clove cigarettes completes the cultural shift.

The land of these Dani is the Grand Valley of the Baliem River, a broad, temperate plain lying 5000 feet above the tropical jungles of New Guinea. At least 50,000 Dani live in the densely settled valley floor, and another 50,000 inhabit the scattered settlements along the steep-sided valleys around the Grand Valley. Temperature is mild, rainfall moderate, wildlife harmless and disease rare; this is surely one of the most pleasant corners of man's world.

It is the only place in the world where man has improved on nature…it is as close to paradise as one could get.

Robert Mitton, *Lost World of Irian Jaya*, OUP, Melbourne, 1983

Jagged quartzite rock ruptures the highest grasslands and winding paths shrouded by trees traverse the edge of the Baliem River. Here, for possibly 25,000 years, the Dani have lived their lives as warriors and farmers.

The traditional dress of the Dani is made entirely from the natural environment. Prior to marriage young girls wear grass skirts; later, their husbands make them skirts of braided bark, dyed deep reds and yellows with coloured orchid fibres. Long string bags, *noken*, heavy with the smell of smoke from village fires, hang from the top of the head down to the back of their knees. *Noken* are decorated with vegetable dyes and used to carry both sleeping children and vegetables from the garden. The men traditionally wear only penis gourds, which grow on native vines, and sometimes upper arm bracelets made of rolled bark. Ceremonial clothing includes pig tusks worn through the nose, long ties made of tiny cowrie shells and body paint. Their hair is rolled and oiled with pig fat.

The Indonesian government tried to enforce Operation Koteka—*koteka* being the Indonesian word for gourd—to formally ban traditional dress. The government maintained the view that it was primitive and the Dani must learn to wear modern clothes. Resistance was so great that the government was forced to abandon the operation. However, as years have passed, young Dani have increasingly adopted modern clothing.

Nearly 100,000 Dani people live in the Baliem, a beautiful valley in the middle of West Papua. Sixty kilometres long, 15 kilometres wide and surrounded by 3000-metre high peaks, it is laced with intricate and precariously hanging gardens.

Through this highland valley courses the Baliem River. Fast flowing and fed by numerous waterfalls, it provides an important water source for the Dani's complex irrigation networks. Along the alluvial plain sweet potato, taro, yams, ginger and tobacco are all successfully cultivated.

There was a time when the Dani traded only in cowrie shells, pigs, axe heads, stones, furs, feathers and fibres. These days many sell their produce for cash which is often used to buy imported goods from the Indonesian vendors at Wamena markets. In the early morning, Dani women and children sit on the muddy earth selling yams, vegetables, garlic and peanuts, while Indonesian stall holders light their gas stoves to heat bowls of noodles, fried bananas and thick, sweet Indonesian coffee.

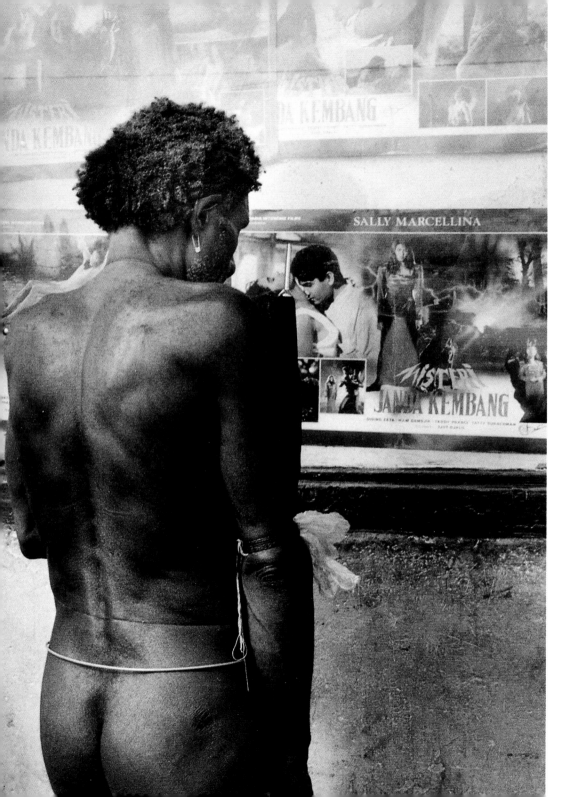

It is quickly apparent who controls the material wealth in the region. All hotels, restaurants and business operations in Wamena are owned by Indonesians or expatriates.

Billboards and posters advertise sexually explicit Indonesian films, a new cultural experience for the Dani.

Leaving Wamena with a guide, porter and a cook, we commence a trek into the Miagima area of the Baliem. Walking along the dirt tracks which lead past the extensive rice paddies toward the outskirts of the town, we reach the fast-flowing Baliem River. Elaborately constructed vine bridges provide a way across the water and to the path which will carry us further into the valley.

After a day's walk along narrow tracks surrounded by dense vegetation, we reach Elegeima Village where we intend to camp for a few days. Dani immediately arrive and help us pitch our tents. An old man sits on a small hillock and softly plays a jew's harp, another rolls a cigarette of local raw tobacco. The community, like all Dani communities, lives in a hamlet or compound. Each compound is surrounded by a retaining wall within which the Men's House sits at one end and is bordered by the women's circular huts and one long cooking hut with a separate area for the pigs.

Built of hardwood and held together with vine or bamboo lashings, the huts are divided into two floors and have heavily thatched grass roofs. In the centre of the lower level a continually smouldering fire is surrounded by four polished posts. In the early morning, as the mist rises, smoke filters its way through the thatch and smothers the roof in a thick white hovering blanket. Small green plants and gourd vines also erupt from the thatch, creating a strange, trailing garden. With no windows, light enters the ground floor from the entrance, while the top floor is in complete darkness.

Much of the Dani's time was traditionally spent in the practice of ritualised warfare, however there was no belief in an end to fighting and war was not a means to realise peace. The motivation for battle, rather then the acquisition of land, was generally to placate ancestral spirits, if these ancestors had been killed in war, their deaths must be avenged. For the Dani the 'risks involved in fighting an occasional battle are not nearly as great as those to be encountered were they to ignore the demands of unavenged ghosts.'

R. Gardner and K.G. Heider, *Gardens of War*, Random House, New York, 1968 p 136.

Without it the culture would be entirely different, indeed, perhaps it could not find sufficient meaning to survive.

R. Gardner and K.G. Heider, op. cit., p 144.

Battles were fought between various alliances, of which there were a dozen or so, each alliance spread across an area of about 50 square kilometres. Battles would commence when both sides were ready and during a day's fighting there would be between 10 or 20 clashes. At sunset, fighting ceased and was replaced with verbal abuse hurled across the battleground, which apparently often lead to a great deal of laughter. Late in the evening people would return home. Casualties were generally very few and according to first-hand accounts, the Dani were more concerned with practising tactics and competence in dodging flying arrows than with actually killing each other.

Frontiers established between each alliance were constantly guarded by warriors with bows and arrows standing in tall bamboo and vine watchtowers. The watchtowers were built outside most hamlets to guard against more serious battles which occurred in the form of raids. These were neither pre-arranged nor humorous and the objective was to kill a member of the enemy clan. Unlike a battle, there was no warning or pre-arranged time. Instead, sometimes in the night, men would raid another hamlet with the intention to harm.

When a man was injured, the immediate concern was for the dislodgement of the *etai-eken* (seeds of singing), corresponding to the Western notion of the soul. If blood was spilt and reached the *etai-eken*, it was believed to cause the victim grave harm. A specialist or Dani surgeon was immediately called to perform a ritual incising and another person to speak to the *etai-eken*. By blowing on certain parts of the body, singing and pointing dried grass towards the solar plexus, where the *etai-eken* belong, they were encouraged to return to their proper position.

The Indonesian government banned traditional warfare, a move supported by missionaries who condemned the activity as barbaric. While it has brought peace to the valley, it also has meant that one of the most significant occupations of the men has disappeared with little to replace it. Today most of the watchtowers have fallen down or are in a state of disrepair. The watchtower at Miagima has a washing line tied to it, on which the Dani hang their clothes.

Crossing the river once again, this time on open rafts made from strips of timber strapped to logs and moved across the water with long, flexible poles, we arrive at a nearby village where the villagers bring out one of only three smoked mummies reputed to be left in the valley.

The Dani are animists and their spirit world is intricately bound up with the spirits of their dead relatives who manifest in the form of ghosts. Ghosts are believed to be responsible for most things. The weather, sickness and everyday events are to some degree determined by the influence of ghosts, and sickness or death is often attributed to their displeasure. It is fear of this that keeps the Dani on a constant vigil, making sure that through their magic, they keep the ghosts happy.

Important chiefs were traditionally preserved through a method of smoking over an open fire. Their bodies were kept in special huts and revered by the rest of the village, though this practice no longer takes place. A fee is now required to look at or photograph these ancient relics as the Dani become increasingly aware of the monetary potential of tourists and journalists.

Jabarip, shell strips, are often brought to a funeral, draped around the corpse and removed shortly before cremation. These, along with other belongings of the dead, are sometimes placed inside the hollow of a tree or a small dwelling. It is customary for relatives of the dead person's mother to bring shell objects to the funeral; relatives from the father's side provide pigs—and these items are exchanged.

On certain occasions the bones of a dead chief are placed inside a ceremonial cage.

While walking alone one day, the sound of crying cuts through the early morning and I am drawn to a small compound at the edge of the dirt road. An old woman beckons when she sees me looking through the entrance way. Inside, a dead child has been strapped into a small bamboo chair. Women are crying and touching the body. Men stand in the background close to strips of pig meat, which are hung over long strands of vine, later to be distributed. As one woman begins an intense incantation, several others carry the small chair to the pile of wood and place it on top. Someone stoops to light the fire and flames quickly surround the body. The closest female relatives lie around the fire, their hands repeatedly reaching towards the flames. The sense of loss and sorrow is overwhelming.

Traditionally a small clump of grass is held above the burning body and a tiny arrow shot through. This signifies the releasing of the dead person's spirit. The clump of grass is then placed near the door of the hamlet so that the ghost might leave easily. The largest and most important funerals are conducted for those who died at the hands of the enemy.

To keep the spirits of the dead happy, it is customary for Dani women to have one or two fingers cut off at the knuckle after the death of a close relative. By knocking the elbow, the hand is numbed and then the finger is removed with a small adze. The fingers are put in the ashes of the funeral pyre and the rest of the hand is bound with leaves. For the women who spend most of their time digging in the gardens and are extremely dependent on their hands, this is indeed a great sacrifice. Men sometimes slice off the top of their ears in a similar gesture of mourning and reconciliation with the spirits of the dead. Although almost every adult has experienced a sacrifice, it is less common now and there are few young children who have been subjected to the ordeal.

It's not only the influence of the Indonesians that has had such a crushing impact on traditional Dani culture, but also the missionaries. The arrival of missionaries made a huge impact, not just in the Baliem but all over West Papua. While the older generation of West Papuans rejected Christianity for many years, there is little doubt that it is now taking hold and, as is so often the case, the missionaries remain intent on breaking down traditional spiritual beliefs. However, even if Christian funerals are taking over from the traditional practices, the offerings being brought to this particular church service were bilum bags filled with sweet potato and taro fresh from the gardens.

One of the most visually striking aspects of the Baliem are the incredible gardens which sometimes hang from the sides of mountains, 3000 metres high and so sheer that women tend them holding onto vines. On the valley floor, canals as deep as the Dani are high, have irrigated and drained the thousands of garden plots. Some anthropologists believe the Dani may have developed one of the most sophisticated agricultural systems in the world.

Traditionally crafted adzes or small axes were made of sharpened stone blades attached to a wooden handle with strands of vine. Until recently the Dani lived in a stone-age culture and technology drew exclusively from the natural environment using stone, bone, wood, bamboo and vine. Fire was created by rubbing a bamboo strap under a piece of split hardwood, beneath which lay a small bundle of dry grass that was ignited by the sparks produced through the friction. Since the rapid process of development began, iron and steel implements have become increasingly popular. Steel axes have replaced most of the stone adzes and lighters are used to start fires.

Traditional pig kills are a part of most Dani rituals and ceremonies. In Elegeima Village the entire community prepared for a feast that would last most of the day and all night. Precious cus cus fur headbands and ceremonial penis gourds were unwrapped and bodies painted. Highly prized feather and pig tusk ornaments were put on just as the men returned to the hamlet. The dead pigs were charred on an open fire and the hair scraped from their skin with small sticks. They were then cut up with razor-sharp bamboo knives. The Dani work with great speed and skill, carefully dividing and preparing the meat.

Pigs are not only an essential part of ritual feasts but an important exchange item. They were probably introduced some 5000 years ago and now, as in most of Melanesia, they are considered to be of great value. A sign of wealth and social status, they form part of the bride price the groom will pay. Pigs are used at funerals, victory celebrations, marriages and religious ceremonies, and also as a form of compensation when required. They are looked after mostly by the women, who are often so close to their pets they have been known to breastfeed orphaned pigs. During ritual feasts, pigs are tied to a pole with vine and killed with a bow and arrow, which often reduces the owners to tears.

Down by the river, Issac, son of the village chief, stood knee-deep in water as elders painted his body with leaves covered in a mixture of lime and ash.

Large stones are placed on top of firewood before the fire is lit. The stones are soon white hot and, using large bamboo tongs, are transferred to a pit dug in the ground and lined with grass. Once a layer of stones has been arranged by the men, the women move forward. Arriving at the hamlet with large bilum bags filled with root vegetables, they smother the rocks and grass with cau cau, taro and sweet potato of all shapes and sizes. These are then covered with a blanket of edible ferns. Once the women have moved away, the men re-enter and place another layer of hot stones over the food. They withdraw and the women reconvene to place another layer of food. This goes on until the pit becomes a mound nearly a metre high atop of which is placed the dismembered pig. The grass lining is pulled up to cover it so the oven eventually looks something like a giant bird's nest. The mound is then secured with vine, sprinkled with water from a dried gourd and left for a few hours.

Ceremonial dancing continues throughout the cooking process. When the food is considered ready, the pit is opened and the contents placed in piles around the fire. Everything is carefully divided and the feast commences. Festivities often continue throughout the night with drums and flaming torches as people dance around the fire. As dancers move away to rest, others come forward to participate and the movement remains continuous for hours.

Feasts were traditionally the sign of either recent death or an attempt to ensure peace after a big war. Small feasts were held after small wars when payment for the dead or wounded was made. Today, as a result of the increasing number of tourists visiting the valley, the Dani will stage a pig kill and feast in their village for around 200,000 rupiah (A$40).

Until recently Wamena was one of the largest towns in the world, serviced only by air—the impact of the outside world was largely restricted to Indonesian military personnel, a handful of transmigrants and an equally small number of tourists. However, over the past decade the Trans-Irian Highway has been completed and bulldozers have torn up the valley and the tarred road skirts the edges of Dani hamlets. Villages reached a decade ago by narrow winding pathways bordered with forests and wildlife are now on the local bus route. The highway connects Jayapura on the north coast with Merauke on the south coast and passes directly through Wamena. Its opening has brought, or will bring with it, a huge influx of new influences and increasing numbers of transmigrants, and will have a dramatic effect on what remains of Dani culture. It will also facilitate the extraction of resources.

The Freeport mine in West Papua sits on part of a mountain range that runs right through the Baliem Valley all the way to the PNG border. It is believed that, like Freeport, the rest of the range holds enormous reserves of copper and gold. Companies, including Freeport, have already been prospecting in the area and leases have been granted for both logging and mining in the Baliem Valley. The completion of the highway provides the necessary transportation facilities. The Dani continue to own their land because it is cultivated, however, the government remains able to extract resources from it, which will inevitably result in serious environmental degradation. The extracting of resources, the use of people's land—without compensation for loss or damage—undermines the basic laws of Melanesian culture and traditional land rights. The violation of traditional land rights was, in the past, one of the major causes of warfare.

On my first trip to the Baliem in 1988 I hardly saw a tourist. A decade later in 1998 we were inundated with guides as we left the airport in Wamena. People with cheap imitation carvings ran along the road behind us as we tried to find a guest house and numerous guides attempted to win us over with financial arrangements. The bus took us to Elegeima village; six years before it had taken a full day to walk through dense vegetation. Tourist numbers are increasing and the remote, exotic cultures that Indonesia promotes as an attraction are in rapid demise. Intent on undermining Dani culture ever since the official Indonesian takeover in 1963, the Indonesians have now changed tack. In 1986 they lifted restrictions prohibiting any kind of tourism and allowed small numbers of tourists to visit specified areas, usually those experiencing minimal unrest. The Baliem Valley, despite the fact there had been serious resistance to Indonesian rule, was relatively quiet compared to other areas. Having recognised that local cultural traditions are of interest to tourists and therefore a potential source of income, Dani culture has become a marketable commodity. T-shirts advertise it as a 'Land of the Unexpected', Indonesian stall holders sell penis gourds and grass skirts and large expeditions are flown into remote areas in order to access communities that have managed to retain some aspect of their traditional lifestyle, though tour groups ensure that this will not remain the case.

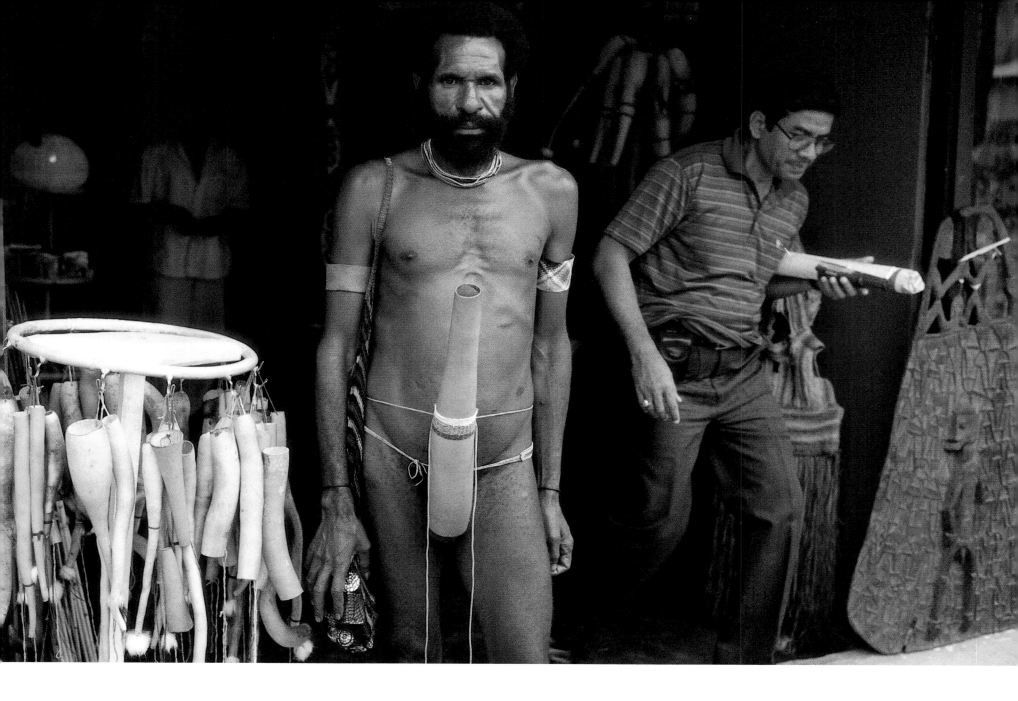

By the year 2000 human society promises to vary little from continent to continent. Transportation and communication will link the remotest valley and farthest plateau with centres of technology. Deserts will be watered and marshes drained, and the cultures that developed in response to isolation and hardship will have disappeared.

R. Gardner and K.G. Heider, op.cit.

As little as 30 years ago the Dani lived in a predominantly stone-age culture—gardening, going to war, practising magic and worshipping ancestral spirits—largely unaware of a world beyond the edges of their own valley.

Today their children go to school, earn cash, travel in buses and wear modern clothes. They use tools made of iron and steel, and are exposed to tourism, missionaries and the Indonesian military. They have experienced the banning of traditional warfare, attempts to ban traditional dress and have found that speaking your mind is often met with torture or imprisonment. Most Dani would know somebody who has died at the hands of the Indonesian military.

Military presence remains strong in Wamena. Asked about the political situation, most Dani are reluctant to speak openly and there is a prevailing sense of fear in relation to the continued military control of the area.

The Asmat is a swampy lowland area on the south-west coast of West Papua. Flying from Wamena in the Baliem Valley to Sengo, a small Asmat township, you can see as the fast-flowing Baliem River leaves the mountains and forms a wide delta across vast mud plains before it finally flows into the ocean.

In his *Lost World of Irian Jaya*, Tony Mitton says that the Asmats believe there are three kinds of human beings; the living, the recently dead and the long dead. It is the recently dead that potentially cause problems for the living in the form of malevolent ghosts, but can be helped to move into the state of long dead by conducting certain rituals. As in all areas of West Papua, the placating of ancestral spirits is of great importance and carries great significance for the well-being of the living. Mitton tells how a dead person would be put on a platform in the bush until the flesh had rotted away and only then would the bones be removed and placed amongst the roots and trunk crevices of a fig tree.

One aspect of the Asmat cultural life which has become somewhat infamous is the practice of homosexual relations between adult men and young boys. The Asmat believe that semen is extremely powerful and sodomy, including the emission of semen into the anus, was part of a young boy's initiation process. It was a widely held belief that this fluid would bring them strength and masculinity. The partnerships established between these boys and adult men often continued for many years.

The Marind were obsessed with semen. They used it in arrows, canoes, gardens and food. They claimed that the holy water used in Roman Catholic services must be ineffectual as it contained no semen. Traditionally dances involved erection and ejaculation into shells and copulation. For the transition rites, semen was spread all over the floor. Father Van de Wouw started many projects to try to get the people's minds off sex and semen: these projects included a brass band and football. The people also used to drink fluids from dead bodies.

Mitton, op. cit.

On walking into a losman (a small guest house) the Indonesian owner, helped by her beautiful young daughter, brings out mugs of tea with tiny lids designed to keep the drink warm. The shelves of the shop are lined with jars and spices. Walking to the police station in the intense heat to register for our *salat jalan* or visas, we find it unattended and sit on the steps while someone tries to nudge the official from his afternoon siesta. The policeman finally shows up and, after some extensive red tape, paperwork and finally bribes, we eventually have our visas.

After organising to hire canoes in which we'll travel down the river, I drink litres of warm water laced with the delicate taste of coconut which has been left to sit in the buckets of rainwater. After a night of dominoes and rum with the local policemen, whose guns are propped up in the corner, we hear the cockerel crow at dawn. Walking to the river along winding pathways, we see women carry fishing nets—large wooden frames from which hang bark rope nets. The women, their nets and the mud are all the same monochromatic colour of the earth. The canoes sit in the murky water and when the necessary police escort arrives, we leave.

After a short period travelling on the water, the river opens out and is lined by thick lush rainforest and impenetrable vines. For hours we travel in the blinding sun. Slowly and mercifully, as the day passes and we move further upstream, the afternoon light grows softer. After a rough night of camping we head further up-river, where the air is filled with the sound of cicadas and the cries of jungle birds. The vegetation creeps to the surface of the river, the sky is blue and empty. Villages and their inhabitants periodically line the banks. Women carry firewood in ochre bilum bags across their backs, heads bowed under the weight of their load. Finally we stop at a village called Patipi. It has approximately 20 huts, each one inhabited by about six people. They say there is no one left in the jungle and that they have all come here because their abandoned village on the other side of the river made of bush materials is slowly disintegrating. Through the window of the local school I see the blackboard on which are lessons listing the names of Indonesian prime ministers and details of the Muslim faith, information which seems wildly incongruous in this jungle environment in which animism has fuelled spiritual beliefs for centuries. The villagers look hungry and many are suffering from skin diseases and malnutrition.

Looking at the old faces we can't help but wonder at the extent of change they have experienced in one lifetime—25,000 years of tradition rapidly giving way to the arrival of the modern world. We talk to one old man, the only one left who had been on a traditional raid to an enemy village many years ago. He was a small boy at the time and describes how the raid took place in a village two days journey up-river and which is now abandoned. Ten men took part and killed five men. They took the women back for wives. The old man shows with his hands how they dissected the bodies; cutting off the arms and legs, and with a sweeping movement of his hands, showed how they split the stomach from neck to pelvic bone. His actions become more dynamic as his memory is evoked. They stabbed the enemy in the neck with a cassowary bone dagger and the dismembered bodies were taken back to their village and eaten, the skulls thrown into the river. Suddenly most of the village appears brandishing bows and arrows, pulling the strings and letting them slam forward, jumping up and down in a strange position, knees and elbows outstretched and repeatedly brought into the sides. The kind of gesture you'd use to mimic a chicken, all of this accompanied by loud whooping. Shields fly in the undergrowth, held by unseen bodies, and they become animate amidst the ferns and jungle palms. The whooping continues and it's easy to imagine the terror this scene would have inspired on a raid. Fortunately, they're having a joke at our expense on this occasion, inspired by our discussion with the old man.

In the early morning we follow three tiny dugout canoes to the opposite bank of the river. Two families are going to collect sago, the staple food of many villagers in both PNG and West Papua, particularly in lowland river systems. One man begins to chop at the chosen palm, accompanied by a communal chant which reverberates through the vegetation. The tree falls and the real activity begins. Fronds are broken from the palm, the bark is pounded until it loosens and is cut away to reveal a deep red and amber skin. The flesh is pounded with an axe made of wood and vine until it shreds and spills out from the trunk, landing on the deep green leaves that have been placed on the ground. A woman carefully cuts upper sections from the palm, digging out the milky white palm heart which is immediately eaten in large chunks. Branches are tied with vine, forming supports, and the leaves are created into a tube-like shape. The tree's fibrous material is pegged across the inside of the tube with bamboo clips and serves as a filter. Smaller branches and supports follow until it is perhaps three metres in length and the final structure is plugged with sago clippings. Holes are dug in the swampy ground which soon fill up with water. A woman with a baby strung across her back in a bilum bag places a bowl of pulp in the upper tube and pours water across it, squeezing it intermittently. The water flows white, filled with starch which settles in the bottom rung of the sago washing system. This process continues until all the pulp has been washed, the fluid is left until the starch has settled. Finally the stopper is removed and the fluid drained. leaving a thick white starch in the base. The starch is made into brick shapes and covered with dry palm fronds which are then set alight. This dries out the surface of the sago and makes it easier to transport. The top crusty layer is peeled off and passed to us to taste; it's sweet, hot and glutinous. We leave the site, the small factory erected and abandoned in a morning's work, and everyone is in high spirits. The blocks are packed into bags and we walk through the jungle on freshly laid palm fronds and wash the sweat and insects off in the cool flow of the river.

Government and missionaries have discouraged traditional body adornment. Some of the older people wear small wooden spikes in their noses—the women four, men usually six. Most wear nothing but the small circular scars on their noses that bear witness to the recent demise of a tradition. Through an interpreter, villagers tell of having their ornaments taken from them and thrown into rivers, their traditional practices outlawed and their art work destroyed. So fearful are they of losing their heritage completely they have hidden what little remains deep in the jungle.

The rich collection of Asmat carvings is now greatly reduced. The superb traditional shields used in warfare and raids, decorated with designs of flying foxes, cus cus, bats and birds have mostly been either destroyed or shipped out to museums and private collections. Many are in Indonesia. The artistic traditions of the Asmat were broad and included sculpted carvings—which both protected the community from malevolent spirits and encouraged benevolent influences—and decorated paddles and canoes. They also included the creation of certain masks or costumes. The pokman, a woven mask with waistbands and epaulet arm adornments, hung with grass skirts and long pieces of dried grass covering the arms, were banned by the Indonesian government as symbols of head-hunting. The masks and costumes were highly sacred and only brought out for ritual purposes. In most instances, women and small children were not included in sacred ceremonial practices. The Asmat were not, from all accounts, a particularly egalitarian society.

The production of Asmat art work is now encouraged only from a commercial point of view and used to feed the tourist market. West Papuan culture is valued and condoned by the Indonesian government only when it serves as a lucrative financial enterprise.

Loggers plunder the local resources. Land is taken with little or no compensation to settle Indonesian transmigrants. The proud naked bodies of the Asmat people are now dressed in ragged western clothing, dirty and ripped. Their jungle homes have been replaced with institutional rows of regimental wooden houses which they have been encouraged to move into by government representatives. The designs take little account of traditional living practices. Nobody seems to spend any time inside the houses, all sitting out in the open around small fires smoking long wooden pipes.

The government and missionaries claim to have civilised the Asmat, as they claim to have improved the lot of all West Papuans. On the contrary, for most West Papuans their quality of life and their sense of dignity and empowerment has significantly deteriorated. There remains a widespread resentment among West Papuans over the presence and rule of Indonesians. They remain committed to the independence movement and continue the struggle to secure self-determination for the West Papuan people.

The Irianese could cope, despite all that was stacked against them by the government, with development that was sensitive and gradual, and designed to help them, not destroy them. If the government had spent a fraction of its transmigration money, seven and a half billion dollars, on the gentle development of the Irianese, they might willingly have jumped at the chance of change.

George Mombiot, *Poisoned Arrows*, Abacus, London, 1989. p 236.

Ben Bohane

If someone comes into your garden and steals your pig, does not tell you or offer any compensation, then you have a right to kill them. That is tribal law.

OPM Commander Titus Murip

It was late at night when the elders of Ngselema village woke me, beckoning me to the main room of the Men's House. Outside, pigs grunted and the faint sound of mouth harps twanging in nearby huts was carried in the cool, mountain air. As oil lamps flickered I could make out two dozen or so old and weather-beaten faces peering at me through the dark. There, laid out on the floor in front of me, were 10 or 12 items. Slowly, reverently, Silas, who was wearing a wallaby head-dress, picked up each item to explain it to me. 'This is a koteka (penis gourd) for men', 'this is assgrass (grass skirt) for women', 'this is pandanus leaf for making thatch roof', 'this is a carved arrow for hunting cassowary'. He paused lovingly on each item, seeing that I had taken it in. At first I was a bit bemused. This was all pretty self-explanatory, I thought. Why had they bothered to make a ceremony out of it? But it slowly dawned on me that what they were displaying was the sum total of their material wealth as a culture. These 12 simple items had sustained countless generations of people for thousands of years.

I was immediately struck by the marvel of that, how a society could survive and flourish in such a wild landscape with so little. But Silas wasn't finished yet. He picked up two other items which were displayed as if additions to their culture. One was a chunk of rock with bright little flecks on it, representing the wealth of copper and gold that lay in their earth. The second was a bible, emphasising the most important foreign addition to their culture, an addition which they prized highly but was still mysterious to them, as if it was an instruction manual that they hadn't quite got the hang of yet. Looking into Silas' eyes, there seemed something questioning, confused almost. When he and the others spoke, they implied that all this had been enough to sustain them over the years, that they had lived freely according to their timeless ways and been able to defend their traditional lands. No longer. What Silas and the elders were saying was that what they had was not enough anymore. Their lands were being exploited by others for fabulous wealth, their people were being attacked by Indonesian troops and they could feel themselves been squeezed out of their traditional land, unable to defend it as in days past. The look on their faces betrayed a sense of fear, of sadness, for their very future. Less than 100 kilometres away from our hut, the 24-hour-a-day operation of Freeport copper and gold—the largest, most advanced gold mine on earth—was grinding ore in the night. The contrast between this billion dollar, space-age mining project planted in their midst and the 12 bare items laid out on the floor in front of me could not have been more extreme.

'We must have our independence', Silas said finally, and everyone nodded their heads in silence.

Village elder holds a chunk of rock (symbolising the wealth of copper and gold) and a bible, two of the most significant introductions into West Papuan life.

Sometimes a big issue has to be stripped back to its most simple building blocks. In November 1996 I found myself in what is surely one of the last places on earth—the highlands of West Papua—trekking for six weeks with the Central Command of the OPM to interview some of the leaders of this long-forgotten war. In these remote and otherworldly mountains, I remember listening to Commander Titus Murip break down what could be seen as the incredibly complex international geopolitical status of West Papua into the simple prism of tribal law.

Freeport and the Indonesian military were continuing—both literally and metaphorically—to enter their gardens and take their pigs without offering any compensation. Therefore the OPM, defending the interests of local people, had a right to kill them. That is tribal law and the essence of their legitimacy to struggle.

They are either wild terrorist gangs or freedom fighters depending on your viewpoint, but for 40 years groups of wandering OPM guerillas have roamed the jungles, raised their Morning Star independence flag, attacked Indonesian army patrols and tried to educate villagers in the political history of their country and the need to liberate it. Few conflicts on earth have been so comprehensively ignored by the media and regional governments, yet church groups and non-government organisations claim more than 100,000 people have perished from 40 years of Indonesian 'occupation'. What has been going on in this vast and ancient land, whose wilderness is second only in size to the Amazon Basin and lies just spitting distance from Australian shores? Dark murmurs of atrocities and dispossession have been seeping out for decades now. Only rarely has West Papua been thrust into the international spotlight.

In the mid-1960s West Papua gained fame for swallowing up young Michael Rockefeller, heir to the largest fortune in America, when he disappeared on an expedition looking for decorative skulls taken by headhunters in the Asmat area. A failed uprising in the Baliem Valley in 1977 gained attention when it was learnt that the Indonesian military had napalmed whole villages and shot hundreds of people. As a peace gesture, the military later introduced poisoned pigs to unsuspecting villagers. In more recent times, the hostage-taking of four British, two Dutch and a German in 1996 for four months made international headlines. The TNI were handed a public relations victory when OPM Commander Kelly Kwalik refused to hand over the hostages to the Red Cross and two Indonesian hostages were killed.

Then, on 10 November 2001, the President of the Papuan Presidium Council, Chief Theys Eluay, was found strangled in his car after attending a Kopassus military banquet. A state-sanctioned assassination is all but confirmed. The chief had attempted a peaceful, diplomatic approach to the independence issue, but some within the independence movement believe the struggle will only be won through more forceful means.

Having taken something of a backseat when the Papuan Presidium Council was formed in 1999, the OPM is now likely to continue its guerilla activity regardless of what happens in the diplomatic arena.

Although short on weapons, thousands have been trained in the fundamentals of guerilla war. What makes the OPM different from many other liberation groups is its essentially decentralised nature and lack of a unified command structure. Ethnic rivalries, lack of telecommunications and simple geography all play a part in this, so essentially it has been left to regional commanders, sometimes in coordination, often times not, to conduct operations as they see fit. Many have claimed the mantle of Supreme Commander over the years; from Seth Rumkorem and Jacob Prai, to Nicholas Jouwe and, today, Matthias Wenda and John Koknak. But it is perhaps more useful to recognise three main command areas that have been most active in recent decades: Central Command led by Kelly Kwalik, Titus Murip and Daniel Kogeya; Northern Command (along the northern PNG border) led by Matthias Wenda; and Southern Command (southern PNG border) led by John Koknak and Bernard Mawen. In the international arena, some of the prominent spokesmen for the movement include Franzalbert Joku (based in PNG), John Otto Ondawami and Rex Rumakeik (both based in Australia). Then there is the tireless human rights campaigner John Rumbiak, whom some have said is a potential Nobel Peace Prize candidate.

For millennia, Papuans had been lords of their own domain, repelling any invader while maintaining elaborate trade relationships with neighbouring tribes and far-away kingdoms alike. Tribal war and violence were regular features of traditional life, but they were regulated so that 'payback' was never excessive. There seemed to be truly an 'art of war' concept which was measured, even chivalrous, in its implementation. In the highlands, particularly, this was so; once an aggrieved party was avenged with the death or wounding of someone opposing them, the battle was usually called off. The idea of war as annihilation of your enemy—the hallmark of many conquering western and Asian armies—seems a largely foreign concept to many Papuans of the interior. But since the UN Act of Free Choice handed West Papua to Indonesia in 1969, Papuans feel they have become essentially a subject people. Today their lands remain invaluable to outsiders, providing one of the last great resource bonanzas left in the region. For Indonesia there is land to cultivate and resettle its poor from the overcrowded islands of Java and Sumatra. Plus the returns from Freeport, Indonesia's single largest taxpayer. In another country, such resources would be seen as a blessing, but in West Papua many can see it only as a curse.

Having travelled with numerous resistance groups over the years, what has struck me about the nature of West Papuan resistance is that, despite their complete isolation, lack of military equipment or external support, their determination is as real as any other national liberation struggle in history. It has become a cliché to say that the OPM is 'a state of mind' for most Papuans, but it is quite apparent that the struggle is seen in the deepest spiritual terms as much as a political one, which remains a rather abstract concept for many. Some observers have remarked that the independence movement has taken on an almost a cargo cult-like fervour. This is not to be dismissive;

the reverence with which the Morning Star flag is unfurled is itself an offering to the gods and many successful independence movements throughout Melanesia have had their roots in messianic movements. The assassination of Chief Theys has ensured his place in history as but the latest incarnation of the prophet Mansren, who is constantly reborn in West Papua to help liberate his people.

The greatest challenge, however, may yet prove to be not the Indonesian military but the ethnic rivalry within West Papua. What unifies them, though, is a perceived sense of collective injustice under the status quo. Although many are uneducated by Western standards (or Eastern for that matter), their intrinsic humanity tells them that what continues to be perpetrated against them is fundamentally wrong and that they deserve better. The word 'dignity' pops up often in conversation, as does a desire to express their identity freely. The struggle is particularly profound given the remoteness of their land and the lack of access to information from the outside world. That they are waging this campaign with such little material is in itself an emotional statement. No doubt aware of the odds stacked against them, including the juggernaut Indonesian state and its allies in Canberra and Washington, there is little outward display of fear, prepared as they are to take on the might of the Indonesian military with bows and arrows and a handful of bolt-action rifles. What balances the odds is their bushcraft and ease in this terrain. They will say yes, the Indonesians have the guns, but we have the land: the jungles, mountains and rivers that hide them and sustain them. It is their best weapon and perhaps only defence.

'Wah, Wah, Wah!' You hear them first, a distant chorus rising up from the next mountain range as they pound along jungle trails towards the village. Suddenly they break through a clearing and charge onto a ridge beside a bush church. The men are naked except for penis gourds, smeared in pig fat and ochre colours, some in elaborate cassowary and bird of paradise headdresses and armed with spears, bows and arrows. The women follow in grass skirts, carrying children and bilum bags full of sweet potatoes. 'Wah, Wah, Wah.' The reception from host villagers and other arrivals is just as loud; soon hundreds of tribesmen and women are running around each other in concentric circles, whooping it up through a torrential downpour. Through the melee of shrill whistles and clattering bows and arrows, pigs roam and bonfires crackle as river rocks being heated for earth ovens explode. For several days Amungme, Nduga and Yali people have trekked across 3000-metre mountain ranges to reach this remote village in the heart of the Lorenz National Park. They have come to hear leaders from OPM's Central Command talk on their behalf and raise the independence flag.

For most mountain communities, the outside world comes to them once a week via MAF, the missionary airline which services dozens of little landing strips all over the country. In the highlands it is a lifeline, bringing food, medicine, mail and education to remote communities which receive nothing from the Indonesian state. In Freeport's 2.5 million hectare concession area, which stretches from present operations across the entire Carstenz mountain range to Ok Tedi in PNG, the mountain people see two agendas at work. One is to relocate them from the mountains so the range can be mined. The second is that by moving them, the OPM is denied sanctuary.

OPM independence flag-raising ceremony, Bewani, PNG border.

OPM guerillas sing their national anthem as the Morning Star flag is raised at a camp in the Northern Command, close to the PNG border.

The mountains surrounding Freeport and the Baliem Valley contain the highest peaks in the Pacific, including the only other equatorial glaciers in the world besides Mount Kilimanjaro in Africa. Gazing out of the cockpit window at the expanse of jungle and mountain, it is not hard to see how limited the campaigns against the OPM in this vast green sanctuary must be. In the past, the campaigns have generally been in 'payback' form: if the OPM ambushed an Indonesian army patrol or attacked the mine, the Indonesian military would often respond by selecting several Papuan villages and wiping them out. Such scorched-earth policies have only further entrenched Papuan resentment.

At several points we fly through mountain gorges instead of over them, before the gentle corkscrew landing onto a grass strip carved out of the side of a mountain. Once on the ground I meet Daniel Kogeya, the military Commander for Central Command. He dispatches some letters into the bush and within a day or two we also trek into the bush so I can interview the elusive Kelly Kwalik and other leaders. We begin trekking with a unit of eight guerillas, plodding through dense jungle and eucalypt forest, up large river systems with fast, cascading water. Nearly a week later we are still moving along narrow trails and rope suspension bridges and we come to a ridge where, on a clear day, they say you can see Australia. The men rest on their bows and stand around smoking bush tobacco, gazing out to an azure expanse of sea. When we reach the designated village there is no sign of Kwalik or any leaders, so I am ceremoniously put in a hut to wait. And wait. Days turn into weeks, weeks into a month. Where are they?

Finally, one night, they usher me into the Men's House where a circle of leaders are sitting. Daniel Kogeya breaks the silence. 'First we want to apologise to you for waiting for so long, but we wanted to travel with you for one moon before we felt we could trust you. There has been much killing and Kelly Kwalik and others have lost many of their families, so we have to be careful. But now we want to open our hearts to you.' With that, one of the men seated next to me, Titus, who had travelled with me the whole time, scribbled on a piece of paper and handed it to me. It said 'Kelly Kwalik'! At the time I had no reason not to believe him. After all, there were no photos in existence of Kwalik and no journalist had ever ventured into the Central Command area before. Only later would I learn that he was not Kwalik but Commander Titus Murip, Kwalik's deputy, who had decided to take on the role of spokesman in this situation.

Murip spoke through an interpreter: 'We have heard about Amungme people who were forced to move down into the lowlands away from the mine. Within two years nearly one-third of them had died from malaria. We mountain people have no resistance to malaria.' Murip insisted that his people would fight to remain in the mountains, threatening to kill any mine surveyors who entered their lands. 'The mountains are our mothers, our ladies. Freeport is married to our mountains but they have never paid the bride price,' he said. Their list of grievances is extensive, from pollution concerns at the 100,000 tonnes of mine tailings dumped into the river every day, to anger that less than 10 per cent of Freeport employees are local and those who generally do menial work.

Under Indonesian law there is no government obligation to pay compensation for traditional land taken 'in the national interest' and no legal avenues to stop it being taken away. 'There have been new concessions, new killings, new companies, but no-one has asked the mountain people. The contract should be re-negotiated, with Papuan leaders involved.' OPM leaders say there have been numerous attempts at dialogue with the mine, which mine owners have usually rebuffed, despite attacks over the years, including the attack on slurry pipelines in 1977 which made headlines and cost the company millions of dollars.

The next three days are carnival days, filled with smoke and strange noises, apparitions of tribesmen in ghostly ochre and women splashed in the mud of mourning. It culminates in a military parade of 400 guerillas, a flag-raising ceremony and a speech by Murip and Kogeya. Twenty-five pigs are slaughtered for a feast with taro, pumpkin and sweet potato. At night the makeshift shelters for a thousand guests are turned into emporiums for elaborate story-telling and music, twanging mouth harps and string guitars rising above the cacophony of voices and fires. They believe that the spirits of their ancestors live in the mountains and through the monsoonal rain and wild dances. I couldn't be sure if I wasn't also watching a ghost people, whose land falls under the shadow of Freeport's concession area.

After a rash of negative publicity relating to its human rights and environmental record, Freeport claims to have changed the way it operates, but most observers say any changes are largely cosmetic. Yet having watched every major mining operation throughout Melanesia come under attack from angry landowners, Freeport must be casting a nervous glance over its shoulder. Its owner, the Elvis-impersonating Jim Bob Mofitt from New Orleans, has found that his previously cosy links to Suharto and cronies are history. Meanwhile, the groundswell of Papuan nationalism only continues to grow.

Whether the West Papuans have a legitimate 'legal' right to struggle for independence is largely irrelevant—it is a reality. As Melanesians, there is no more emotional issue than land and they will continue to fight for it.

At some point it must be left to the UN to peer into the black recess of its own soul to re-examine the sham vote it organised in 1969. It was the UN's first ever 'de-colonisation' operation and remains one of the darkest stains on its history. Until then, we all have a ringside seat to watch the latest conquistadors plunge deeper into the heart of this timeless place.

West Papuans will have their day in the sun. This is contrary to the political position taken by the international community at present, but history is ultimately with them.

Canoes at dusk on the West
Papuan side of the Fly River.

103

West Papuan villagers on the banks of the Fly River. ▲

The Fly River. ◀

OPM guerilla being transported by dugout canoe up the Fly River.

Travelling up the Fly River toward the OPM's Southern Command.

▲ OPM guerillas patrol near the Southern Command headquarters.

▶ OPM guerilla in camouflage patrols the Southern Command.

▲ OPM Commander Matthias Wenda, Bewani, near the PNG border.

▶ Wenda at a secret bush camp near the border town of Vanimo.

John Ondawami confronts
Freeport executive Paul Murphy
at a West Papua conference in Canberra.

Conference delegates from around West Papua gather at the OPM's Southern Command headquarters in April 1999 to forge links between the Presidium Council and the OPM in the border areas.

Fly River, OPM Southern Command.

Commander Bernard Mawen and OPM guerillas travel along the Fly River to their Southern Command headquarters.

Commander John Koknak bangs away at his Remington. ▲

Koknak (left) and Bernard Mawen (right) pose against the backdrop of the West Papuan flag. ◀

Southern Commander Bernard Mawen (right) watches a parade of OPM guerillas in training on the banks of the Fly River.

OPM guerillas drilling
with wooden guns.

Boys watch a captured kingfisher bird tied
to a bunch of bananas in a boat on the Fly River.

Women returning to their homes at their refugee camp on the Fly River.

A Dani man walks through Wamena, against a backdrop of town life and mosque.

Last rights for a Dani man.

Kids play on the airfield in Wamena.

Kids cover their ears as an Indonesian military transport plane unloads rice at Wamena airport.

A Dani man climbs up to a lookout tower in his village in the Baliem Valley.

Shanty towns in Jayapura where many transmigrants have settled.

OPM guerilla from Central Command
in the highlands above Freeport.

A Sanguma (spirit) man welcomes me to his Nduga village.

The Sanguma man with a carving
that has been traded from the
coast up to his village in the highlands.

OPM guerillas perform a war dance in the rain, Central Command in the highlands. ▲

A young boy watches a war dance unfold in Ngselema village. ◀

Commander Titus Murip (centre) stands amid an Nduga war dance.

OPM guerillas from Central Command perform a traditional war dance under teeming rain.

▲ ▶ Boys prepare to go into the jungle to learn bushcraft from their scout leader.

OPM rally in the highlands.

'OPM Merdeka', ('Free OPM') is painted on the back of an OPM guerilla during a flag-raising ceremony in the highlands.

Nduga villagers in the highlands.

A woman and child return from the garden with a bilum of sweet potato.

A woman splashed in traditional mortuary mud in the highlands village of Ngselema.

Women welcome OPM guerillas into their Nduga village in the highlands.

143

Leaders in the OPM Central Command: Daniel Kogeya (left) and Titus Murip (right) at Ngselema village during a flag-raising ceremony.

OPM guerillas assembling during a rally in a highland village.

Three generations of Nduga highlanders.

Commander Titus Murip and his dingo cross a footbridge in the highlands.

Nduga tribesmen prepare a pig feast during an OPM rally in Central Command.

An OPM guard with cassowary headdress during an OPM rally in the highlands.

Traditional raincoats in the highlands.

An OPM guerilla poses against a mountain backdrop in the highlands.

Jim Elmslie

Jim Elmslie is a political economist and tribal art dealer who has studied and worked on the island of New Guinea since 1983. For ten years he operated a lodge on the Sepik River in conjunction with the local people, and took trekking groups to the Baliem Valley in West Papua. He has also worked on feature films, documentaries and advertising shoots throughout the island. In 2001 he completed his Doctorate in Economics from the University of Sydney entitled 'Irian Jaya Under the Gun: Indonesian Economic Development Versus West Papuan Nationalism'. He is Business Editor with *The Pacific Weekly Review* in Vanuatu.

Liz Thompson

Liz Thompson is a photographer, writer, radio producer and filmmaker. Her films include *The Last Magician*, *Breaking Bows and Arrows*—which won the United Nations Media Peace Award for Best Television in 2002—and *Cave in the Snow*.

Liz has travelled extensively in the Asia–Pacific region. She has regular photographic exhibitions and her articles have appeared in publications including *Australian Geographic*, *GEO*, *The Australian*, the *Sydney Morning Herald* and *Good Weekend* magazine. For over 12 years she has produced radio features for ABC Radio National and Radio Australia, including 'Radio Eye', 'Earthbeat', 'The Listening Room', 'Encounter', 'Arts Today', 'Life Matters' and 'The Spirit of Things'.

In the past seven years Liz has written ten books, including *Aboriginal Voices*, *From Somewhere Else* and the series *Fighting for Survival*, which was nominated for the Australian Awards for Excellence in Educational Publishing and the Children's Book Council's Information Book of the Year Award. In 1996 Liz worked as an official photographer when His Holiness the Dalai Lama visited Australia to conduct the Kalachakra Initiation Ceremony. Her photographs were used in *Images*, a book produced to record the event.

Ben Bohane

Ben Bohane is a photojournalist who has been covering events in the Asia–Pacific region for over 14 years.

Much of that time has been spent covering events in Melanesia. He has covered every major conflict and political crisis in the region from West Papua and East Timor to Bougainville, the Solomons and Fiji. On many occasions Ben has been the first journalist to interview such figures as the BRA leader Francis Ona in Bougainville, leaders of the OPM Central Command in West Papua, leaders of Malaitan Eagle Force in the Solomon Islands and the Commander of Laskar Jihad in Ambon, Umar Thalib. Ben was the only journalist inside the PNG Parliament House when it was under siege by PNGDF Special Forces during the Sandline mercenary crisis. He has worked for many of the world's major news organisations, including time and *Asiaweek* magazines, the *Sydney Morning Herald*, *The Australian*, *The Bulletin*, *South China Morning Post*, *Asahi Shimbun* and various US and European publications. He has also worked on TV current affairs and documentaries for ABC and SBS Television in Australia. Ben is currently based in Vanuatu where he is the Editor of *The Pacific Weekly Review*—the first weekly newspaper dedicated to covering the whole Pacific—which he helped to establish in 2002.